Dyton Owen has a straightforward and compelling way of communicating the essence of what a healthy, balanced church is all about. In four chapters he outlines the basic traits by which every church should be measured. This book is an outstanding resource for pastors, lay leaders, and church members who want their local church to be what God intends the church to be. I recommend it highly.

- **Dr. Clayton Oliphant**, Senior Pastor, First United Methodist Church, Richardson, TX

When I first met Dyton Owen as a teenager he was accompanying his District Superintendent father conducting charge conferences in United Methodist congregations in northeastern Oklahoma. With a constantly growing relationship with his parents, I followed Dyton through years in college and seminary and as he pastored Methodist churches in Oklahoma, Kansas and Nebraska. As I read his clear summary of things in Remembering Who We Are: Four Essential Marks of the Church, *I was reminded of the succinct and clear style his father used in several books which he had authored. Readers of this volume will be richly rewarded.*

- **Bishop John Wesley Hardt**, Bishop in Residence Emeritus, Perkins School of Theology at Southern Methodist University, Dallas, TX

I remember well Bishop Ray Owen. When I was a senior pastor, I used to read his church newsletter articles and later his books. I enjoyed them because he said so much in just a few words. Little stories that helped bring the truth to daily life. This book, by Bishop Owen's son, reminds me of those writings. Dyton appreciates the truth he learned from his father and has a special gift of telling the Gospel story in a fresh, stirring way. I believe that in all of us there is a "core" which unites us as human beings. When we understand that connection and respect it, diversity is not something to avoid but celebrate. My hope is that this book will be a reminder to us that Jesus taught in stories. Thank you, Dyton, for a simply but profound perspective on the Christian story and for respecting your father enough to keep the tradition of sharing the faith alive!

- Dr. Bertha M. Potts, Pastor/District Superintendent (ret.), Oklahoma Conference of the United Methodist Church.

Rev. Dr. Dyton Owen asks an important question of congregations and their leaders: do our churches make "such little difference that if [they] were suddenly gone, no one would notice?" He then explores four essential marks of the Church in this collection of sermons: Kerygma, Koinonia, Diakonia, and Didache. By reminding the Church of its call to share the good news of Jesus Christ, live in fellowship as sisters and brothers, teach the wide span of God's love, and practice self-giving service in the world, Dyton gives us the occasion to reclaim an ecclesial identity grounded in the biblical narrative and the story of salvation history. I recommend this book be used as a resource not simply for reading but for praying that the Church might be renewed in our time and place.

- **Dr. Keith D. Ray II**, Senior Pastor, Clemson United Methodist Church, Clemson, SC.

Remembering Who We Are:
Four Essential Marks of the Church

Dr. Dyton L. Owen

Parson's Porch Books
www.parsonsporchbooks.com

Remembering Who We Are: Four Essential Marks of the Church
ISBN: Softcover 978-1-946478-91-7
Copyright © 2018 by Dyton L. Owen

All rights reserved. No part of this book may be reproduced or transmitted in any form or by any means, electronic or mechanical, including photocopying, recording, or by any information storage and retrieval system, without permission in writing from the publisher.

Remembering Who We Are:
Four Essential Marks of the Church

For Dr. Harrell F. Beck (posthumous)

Professor, friend, mentor.
You befriended me when I was but thirteen.
You inspired me then.
You still do.

Contents

Acknowledgements 13
Foreword 17
Introduction 31
Kerygma 35
Koinonia 43
Didache 51
Diakonia 60
Afterword 69

Acknowledgements

No book is ever a solo project. Even though a single person may write a book, it is not written without the input, influence, encouragement and sometimes criticism of others. Every author ought to be grateful.

That being said, I want to acknowledge my appreciation and gratitude for some of those who have been the most "inputful," insightful, and influential in my life and have made this book possible, often unaware.

My wife, Tammy, has been exactly what I was looking for and more than I ever deserved. When I have dropped the ball, given up or given in, she has stayed with me, encouraged me, been straight with me and, in her own way, spurred me on. I love you, Tammy…thanks for hanging with me and letting me hang with you.

My sincere thanks to Dr. Clayton Oliphant, Dr. Bertha "Bert" Potts, Bishop John Wesley Hardt, (who entered the Church Triumphant in June of 2017), and to Dr. Keith Ray for your kind endorsement of this little book. I count your friendships over the years a great gift.

I have long believed that the ability to tell good stories was the mark of a great preacher. While I do not count myself among the greats, I do consider myself more than fortunate to have as a long-time friend one of the great preachers and storytellers of our day. Dr. James W. "Jim" Moore has been one of the most influential preachers in my life. I have been fortunate to hear him preach on several occasions and I have enjoyed his many books over the years – sometimes more than once. His unique ability to share the Good News through stories has not only captivated the attention of his hearers – including myself – but helped define, in my humble opinion, what good preaching is. His gift of storytelling can be read in the Foreword to this book. I will always be thankful to Jim for taking the time to write the Foreword and, at the same time, captivate my attention again, and for encouraging me.

I do not want to fail to mention my thanks to the following people for their encouragement over many years: Dr. Harrell F. Beck, Professor of Hebrew and Old Testament at Boston University School of Theology, to whom this book is dedicated. Though I was only thirteen when I first met Dr. Beck, he was always eager to hear what was going on in my life over the years and what my plans were for college and beyond. I will always treasure his letters to me and the times we spent catching up over iced tea when we were able to do so. Dr. Robert E. Webber became a friend and mentor while I was working on my doctorate. His big smile and firm embrace always brought a smile to my face and gratitude to my heart. Perhaps the most influential person in my life, after my own father, is Dr. Leonard Sweet. When Len agreed to be my doctoral thesis supervisor some years ago, I was ecstatic! But I quickly began asking myself "What have I gotten myself into?" Len was far more gracious with me in the process of my doctoral work than I deserved. I will always hold Len as one of my dearest friends and biggest "Barnabas forces" in my life. Dr. Thomas Jay Oord has proven to be one of the most influential theologians/philosophers I've had the pleasure of knowing. Talking with Tom is like a breath of fresh air in an environment that is often stagnant and stale. His teaching and books have helped me clarify my own thinking on several topics, and I will always be grateful. Last, but certainly not least, my own father, Bishop Ray Owen. Words are not adequate to express the role dad has taken in my life and ministry. I can only say about dad what the great black preacher/philosopher/educator Howard Thurman once said about an influential person in his life: "He held a crown above my head, and I tried to grow tall enough to wear it."

Finally, thank you to the members of the congregations I have served, and those who have attended seminars and have listened to these words in the form of sermons and lessons. Your kind words and encouragement have been appreciated and uplifting. Every preacher likes to hear that a sermon or lesson proved helpful in some way.

If the thoughts contained herein prove beneficial to someone somewhere, I will have been amply rewarded.

Foreword

Upon this rock I will build my church.
Matthew 16:13-20

A group of birds got together one day and decided to establish a church. A meeting was called so that they might discuss the matter, and decide what they wanted in their church, what was most important and what their church should be.

The Parrot stood and said: "If we are going to have a church, we've got to have organization. We need committees, sub-committees, officers and lots of them. Yes, no question about it... organization is the single most important thing in the church today."

The Pheasant jumped up and said: "I disagree. Organization is all right, but it's much more important to have lots of big, sparkling social events. We all have beautiful feathers and surely God meant for us to show them off. Yes, the most important thing in the church is lots of big, sparkling social events."

The Sparrow chimed in: "No! It's a popular minister. That's what we need the most. Doesn't matter what he says or does so long as he doesn't ruffle anybody's feathers. Yes, a popular minister... that's the most crucial thing."

The Starling shouted out: "Well, I think you are all wrong. Most important of all is to have a beautiful building..."

Next, the Mockingbird spoke up: "We need a minister who is good with young people. That's the key thing... to straighten out these wild young people and keep them off the streets."

Then, the Cardinal (who had just flown in from St. Louis) said: "Well, I think we need a baseball team. The most important thing of all is to have a good baseball team to represent our church. That is vital!"

Well, it was glaringly obvious that there was widespread disagreement as to what was most important in the church. But, just then the wise old Owl slowly stood to his feet... and all grew quiet as he prepared to speak, for he was noted for his wisdom. Reassuringly, the wise old Owl spoke, and he said: "Despair not my friends for we can have all these things." The other birds obediently chimed in: "All these things!" "Yes, we can have all these things!"

They congratulated each other, they shook hands, they

patted each other on the back and thus, they formed their church. And when they got through, do you know what they had? That's right! They had a church for the birds! "A Church for the Birds"... not because of what they had included, but because of what they had left out! "A Church for the Birds"... because there was no good news, no message of God's grace... indeed, no regard for God at all. It was a "Church for the Birds" because there was no sense of mission, or morality, no compassion for others, no thought of sharing the Savior's love, no understanding of service, and no commitment to Christ, no challenge toward Christ-like living.

Now, of course we know that it helps to be organized, it's good to have social events, it's wonderful to have a capable staff and a beautiful facility. But these things become significant only when they spring forth from our commitment to Jesus Christ. These things become significant and sacred only when they enable us to do the work of Jesus Christ.

A few years ago, at Annual Conference, Bishop Ben Oliphint quoted the noted jazz musician Fats Waller. Fats Waller's father was a minister and Fats Waller (wanting to help his dad) would write gospel hymns to sing in church. One of his hymns had this line:

"Everything that's not of Jesus will go down!" This is uniquely true of the church. If you build a church that's not of Jesus, that's not caught up in the spirit and mission of Jesus Christ, it will not last, it will not endure, it will go down!

That is precisely what this remarkable passage in Matthew 16 is all about. What a powerful scene this is. Jesus is about ready to head toward that show-down in Jerusalem. He decides to check out the progress of His disciples. Do they really understand what's happening? Do they really understand what awaits them in Jerusalem and beyond? Do they really understand who He is? So, He stops and asks them: "Who do people say that I am?" They answer: "Well, some say you are John the Baptist and others say Elijah and others Jeremiah or one of the prophets."

Then Jesus asks them that powerful, personal question that has resounded across the ages: "But who do *you* say that I am?" Simon Peter (always the ready spokesman) says: "You are the Christ, the Son of the Living God!!!" Jesus then says this: "Blessed are you Simon Bar-Jona! For flesh and blood has not revealed this to you, but My Father who is in heaven. And I tell you, you are Peter and upon this Rock I will build my church."

Now, what is going on here? What rock is Jesus talking about? What does this mean? It means... that Rock-Solid Commitment to Christ is the only sure foundation for any church! If you have that Rock-Solid Commitment to Christ, your church can withstand any storm. If you don't have that, your church will not last. It will have no staying power. It will either be ripped apart by the hard storms of life without, or it will crumble and fall apart because of decay within. Or, as Fats Waller put it in his gospel hymn "Everything that's not of Jesus, will go down."

Now, let me be more specific and bring this closer to home. Look with me now at three very special qualities that are always found in the firm foundation on which the church must be built.

I. FIRST OF ALL, THERE IS THE ROCK OF FAITH... THE ROCK OF FAITH IN CHRIST.

Lou Holtz is a great motivational speaker. He is in demand all over the country. One of his favorite stories is about a man who accidentally ran his car into a ditch out in the country. The man was not hurt at all, but he was stuck and couldn't get out. He asked a farmer for help. The farmer said: "I have an old mule named Dusty. I think he can pull you out." The farmer hooked Dusty up to the car and when all was ready, the farmer snapped the reins and shouted: "Pull Jack! Pull Joe! Pull Tom! Pull Dusty!"

Amazingly, that old mule named Dusty pulled the car out of the ditch with relative ease. The car owner was impressed and grateful. He thanked the farmer profusely and then he said to the farmer: "Let me ask you something: Why did you call Dusty by four different names?" The farmer said: "Well, you see, it's like this. Old Dusty's eyesight is just about gone and if he thought for a minute that he was the only one pulling, he wouldn't have tried at all!"

The faith that holds the church together and keeps the church going is rooted in the good news that we are not alone! Unlike Dusty, we really have somebody helping us. Christ is with us. We can count on that. And we can count on Him. He is our strength. He is our comforter. He is our salvation. We can face anything because He is with us. Remember how He put it: "Lo, I am with you always even to the close of the age!"

Let me tell you something: I am sold on the church! Do you know why? Because...

There is no institution in the world that serves people

like the church. There is no institution in the world that helps families like the church. There is no institution in the world that redeems lives like the church. There is no institution in the world that teaches love like the church. There is no institution in the world that lifts God up like the church, and there is good reason for that... it's because there is no institution in the world that has Jesus Christ like the church.

The world is starving to death for Jesus Christ and we have Him. That's the bottom line. We are here as people of faith to share Jesus Christ with a needy world and everything we do is for that purpose. We have worship services and Sunday School classes. We have prayer groups, support groups, Bible Study groups, youth groups, children's groups, singles groups, senior adult groups, and mission work groups. We take trips, we put on dramas, we play games, we present concerts, we paint houses, we build clinics, we feed the hungry, and we help the needy. All for one purpose: so we can share the love and presence of Jesus Christ, so we can tell people about Him.

Christ is with us. That's what is right with the Church... and that is our sure foundation... our rock of faith.

II. SECOND, THERE IS THE ROCK OF HOPE.

Not long ago, we received a greeting card at our house. On it was printed a poignant poem that I had never seen before. It touched me. Listen to these beautiful words:

"There have been angels in my life. While they haven't arrived with a blast of trumpets or a rustle of wings, I've known them just the same."

They performed their acts in human guise, sometimes borrowing the faces of family and friends, sometimes posing as well-meaning strangers.

You have known them, too, when just the right word was needed, when a tiny act of kindness made a great difference, or perhaps you heard a voice whispering in a night of sorrow, the words not quite clear, but the meaning unmistakable. "There is hope! There is hope!"

Many of you know well the name of Jackie Robinson. He was one of the greatest baseball players of all time. He was the first African-American to play in the major leagues. He broke the color barrier and because of that lived under incredible pressure. Bigotry screamed at him from every direction. Prejudicial insults came his way daily. Horrible obscenities were shouted at him constantly. He received all kinds of hate mail and all kinds of death threats.

One day he received a particularly disturbing telephone call with a violent threat just before he took the field. It unnerved him, and that day Jackie Robinson was so shaken by the pressure and the threats that he lost his focus (and for one of the few times in his life) was having a bad game. He struck out with the bases loaded. And then shortly after, made a fielding error at second base. The crowd began to boo him unmercifully.

Pee Wee Reese, his teammate, called "time-out." He went over and put his arm around Jackie Robinson and said: "Jackie, let me tell you something. I believe in you. You are the greatest ball-player I have ever seen. You can do it. I know that... and I know something else. One of these days you are going into the Hall of Fame. So, hold your head up high and play ball like only you can do it." A few innings later, Jackie Robinson got the hit that won the game for his team, the Brooklyn Dodgers.

Some years later, when Jackie Robinson was indeed inducted into Baseball's Hall of Fame, he remembered that moment: "Pee Wee Reese was my friend," he said. "He believed in me. He saved my life and my career that day. I had lost my confidence and Pee Wee picked me up with his words of encouragement. He gave me hope when all hope was gone!"

We in the church are called to be "Angels of Hope" to one another like that, yet even more so because our hope is not built upon our ability. No, as the hymn-writer put it, "Our hope is built on nothing less than Jesus' blood and righteousness... On Christ the solid rock we stand, all other ground is sinking sand." First, there is the Rock of Faith, second, there is the Rock of Hope,

and...

III. <u>THIRD AND FINALLY, THERE IS THE ROCK OF LOVE</u>.

Lee McKinzie, one of our ministers, had been on sick leave for two months. On April 3, 1995, (a Monday afternoon) Lee had a heart catheterization done at Methodist Hospital. He had been experiencing some tightness in his chest. The "heart cath" went well and the doctor was explaining to Lee that they had found a couple of places that needed attention, but that he was confident that the problems could be corrected in a non-invasive way.

In typical fashion, Lee was joking with the doctor when suddenly things "turned south." Lee began to have double vision, then his words began to slur and then he went into a coma. This is very rare, but somehow a blood clot had broken loose from somewhere and had hit the stem of the brain. Fortunately, the clot began to dissolve on its own. The following evening (Tuesday night), Lee was still in a coma and we wanted him to hurry and wake up. The doctors sensed our obvious concern and said to us the words we needed to hear: "We are expecting Lee to fully recover and we want you to expect that. However, you must understand that when something like this happens, the coma may last one day, two days, three days, maybe even seven days. I know you want him to hurry and wake up and talk to you. We don't know precisely when that is going to happen, but he will come out of it and he will recover."

The next morning, we had our staff meeting. I was explaining all of this to our staff and reminding them to be patient. "We don't know how long Lee will be unconscious, but the doctors are optimistic, and they want us to be optimistic." We then had a prayer and went on with our meeting. About ten minutes later, our volunteer receptionist walked into the room and handed me a note. All eyes were on that note. I stopped the meeting and read it out loud. "Benny just called to tell us that Lee is awake!"

Ron Morris started singing the Doxology and all the staff joined in, and through our tears of joy and gratitude, we sang the Doxology like it had never been sung before... "Praise God from whom all blessings flow..." and I thought to myself: "This is what love is... and this is what the church is all about... Faith, Hope and Love!!!" A church built on the Rock of Faith in Christ and the Rock of Hope in Christ, and the Rock of Love in Christ... cannot fail. It will (by the Grace of God) endure and prevail to the end of time!

In the pages that follow, Dr. Dyton L. Owen, in his creative and imaginative way, will remind us of the calling of the church, the mission of the church, the purpose of the church and, indeed, the necessity of the church. He underscores the church's unique role in preaching the Gospel, teaching the faith, becoming the redemptive fellowship and taking up the Christ-like spirit of service. This is a book for every pastor and lay leader looking for direction in casting a vision for his her or her congregation that is authentic, biblical and doable.

I know you will be blessed for having read it, and thankful for the reminder of who we are as the Church.

Dr. James W. Moore
Minister in Residence at Highland Park United Methodist Church
Dallas, Texas

Introduction

It has been said that there are no original ideas – although I'm not certain who said it. And I'm not sure I completely agree. Although in the case of this book, the saying does have some merit.

Over the past twenty-five years, much talk has been made and many books have been written on exactly what churches ought to do and be. The words "vision" and "mission," and term such as "long range plans" have been tossed about. There is nothing wrong with that. Every church must have a vision and a mission to stay on task, some idea as to what the church is and what the church has been called to do where it is.

But little – if anything – has been written on such a topic that applies to churches of all sizes and locations. Surely, there must be something, some overarching principles or ideas that can guide the Church in her work, regardless of the individual church's vision, mission, denomination, location, or even size.

I believe there is.

I grew up in the United Methodist Church. My father was a pastor, District Superintendent and Bishop. He was – and is – my hero in the faith. It could be safely said that almost everything I know about being a pastor I learned from following him around as he carried out his ministry in those various roles. And, even those things I did not learn directly from him, I learned vicariously, through watching him. Dad was one of the most adaptable people I have ever known. As ministry and church life changed over his nearly 50 years of ministry, I watched him change his style to better adapt to the changing church he served. He was a constant learner and happily took what he learned and used it to make himself a better, more relevant pastor and preacher.

The topic of this small book is a result of seeing my Dad model its contents. From early in his ministry, he believed with all his heart that the Church must be about certain things if it is going to call itself "church" and if it is to be faithful to both its history and calling. But he also believed that the task of the church must be kept ever before the people if the church is going to have a viable and meaningful future.

I watched my father preach, teach, enjoy the fellowship of the church and serve people from all walks of life. This book is the result of his example.

My original choice for the title of this book was *The Business of the Church*. I was reluctant to use such a title, but in a way, that is exactly what I will be talking about. Aside from all the negative arguments about combining "business" and "church," the Church does have some business to which we are called to attend if we are going to be faithful people. I am grateful to Dr. Keith Ray for inspiring the title of this book as it is now. Without knowing it, Keith hit the nail on the head with what I want to accomplish by writing this little book. Our calling must never be forgotten, ignored, dismissed or downplayed. It is something that must always be reclaimed and kept before us, being worked out among and through us every day.

This book was written in part to remind us of who we are as well as Whose we are, and to refresh our memories of those essential marks of the Church that have been a part of who we are and what we are called to do for 2000 years. In the rush to be "relevant" we have often forgotten who we are and lost sight of the fact that being real is the first step to being relevant.

The Church is the unique vehicle through which this work will take place. No other body, organization, group, or agency has the ability – or calling – to be about this work.

It is an awesome calling. It is a frightening challenge. But it is ours. Let us stop making excuses, blaming others, and denying responsibility for what we have often failed to do. Instead, let us take up this calling, this task, and work together to fulfill it. By so doing, we become the church we are intended to be.

Dyton L. Owen
Junction City, KS
Summer, 2018

Kerygma

The shortest distance between two people is a story.
Anonymous

Some years ago, on the front page of a small-town newspaper was the story of a storm that had passed through that rural town a few days prior. The story read: "We are pleased to report that the storm which blew away the Methodist Church last Friday did no real damage to the community."

Now, that should make us stop and think. If the church – your church – were suddenly "blown away," could we say, "No real damage was done to the community"? Does the Church make such little difference that if it were suddenly gone, no one would notice? Or care? Is the task of the Church considered so unimportant and irrelevant that if it were suddenly gone it would cause no real harm to the town? I hope not!

As a matter of fact, the Church is a very vital part of any community. Its primary task is to proclaim God's message to the human race. That message is known as the *Kerygma* (ker-ig-mah). It is a Greek word that simply means "core" or "central message." The kerygma is the central message of God to the world. We call it the "Gospel."

The Church must keep ever before it, the task of telling the Gospel - or the "Good Story" as I like to call it - that God has given us to share. It is the first and foremost task we must keep at hand. All others follow from it. The "Good Story" is the foundation for all other work of the Church. Without this foundation, the Church falters and fails.

So, what is this kerygma...this Good Story? Peter expressed it best in the gospel of Matthew when he said to Jesus: "You are the Christ, the Son of the living God." Or, put another way, the Good Story is this: Jesus Christ is God's Son, the Savior of the world and Lord of our lives.

That, in a nutshell is the kerygma, the Good Story. That is the message the Church has been entrusted to share. And to understand the meaning of Son, Savior and Lord is to realize how greatly the world – and our communities – would suffer if the Church's message were suddenly "blown away."

CHRIST: GOD'S SON

To start, let's look at the implications of the word "Son." In the Son, God has spoken to the world. God has become known in flesh and blood to the human race. In the Son, God has to spoken on a one-to-one basis the good news to a tired and worried world.

In Jesus, the Son, God is discovered for who God really is. It must have been a wonderful feeling for Peter that day when he at last understood who Jesus really was. Granted, he didn't handle that new discovery very well! But his actions were understandable.

For months, Peter and his fellow disciples had heard Jesus referred to as a great teacher, a rabbi and a prophet. They had heard some say Jesus was Elijah returned, or John the Baptist or Jeremiah. In every instance, it was very complimentary to Jesus. But before Caesarea Philippi, where Peter had his great realization and discovery, none of the disciples had figured out just who Jesus really was. They knew he was a unique man. They knew he was a man of many astonishing gifts and powers. They knew he was a man of unmatched grace and compassion. And they knew he was a man of unsurpassed wisdom and knowledge.

It's no wonder Peter didn't handle his discovery very well! The result of his discovery was too much for him to hold. His mind could not comprehend what he had just come to realize.

Someone once said, "Like a prospector who finds the mother lode, or a prisoner who is suddenly freed, Peter acted with stark immaturity."

And it is still a surprising experience to discover God in the Son. Every other discovery or accomplishment pales in comparison. Sir James Simpson was a very well-known scientist of the mid-nineteenth century. Among his discoveries was the anesthetic quality of chloroform. Someone once asked him what he considered his greatest discovery. Without even stopping to think about it, he replied, "The greatest discovery I ever made was that God had come to us in the person of Jesus."

Few of us are likely considered one of the greatest scientific minds of the world, or one of the greatest apostles of the world – yet. But, when in our hearts we fully and finally discover God, we make the greatest discovery of all. That is why the Church's message to the world is something we and the world cannot do without.

CHRIST: THE SAVIOR

Now let's look at the message that is found in the word "Savior." In Christ, God has acted to save the human race.

From the day Adam and Eve were evicted from the garden, to enslavement in Egypt, to wondering in the Sinai desert, to the land of Canaan, God's people seem to be headed for destruction by their sinfulness. Life had become for them a game of survival. Life never seemed to move upward, but always downward.

In his book of some years ago entitled *Mystery Religions and Christianity*, Samuel Angus wrote, "Prior to the coming of Jesus, it had been centuries of uninterrupted miseries. Men [sic] were looking for salvation from whatever quarter." The world to which God came in Jesus was a world in desperate need of salvation. And it still is!

Jesus came into the middle of all our sin and ugliness and bore it on his shoulders and died with it on the cross not to change God's attitude toward God's people. He died to demonstrate that God's attitude all along has been one of grace and forgiveness. And ever since that day, sin holds influence in our lives only with our permission.

Guilt from past sins may still hold us. It may still be leaving its shame and regret. While in exile, Napoleon Bonaparte sat looking at a map of the world. Pointing to the British Isles, he said, "Were it not for that one red spot, I would have conquered the entire world."

It is always those "little red spots" that cause our guilt. It is always those spots that remind us that we badly need to be rescued. But God cannot do it alone. God will not force it upon us. God cannot make us want to be saved. And God cannot do it unless we invite it.

But on any given day, at any given time, all those spots can be forever removed.

That's the message of the Church we are to share.

CHRIST: THE LORD

Finally, let's look at the part of the Good Story that is found in the word "Lord."

The word "Lord" refers to someone who has power and authority. It refers to one who is in charge of someone else.

When we, the Church, call Jesus "Lord," we are saying that he has power and authority. It is Jesus' Lordship that directs our lives.

As Jesus knelt to wash Peter's feet, the fisherman said, "You will never wash my feet." Jesus answered, "If I do not wash your feet, you cannot be one of mine."

At that moment, Peter made Jesus Lord of his life. Peter said, "Lord, then not only my feet and hands, but my head as well."

No other "Lord" will do for us, either.

You may remember a television show from the mid-1980s to the mid-1990s called "Lifestyles of the Rich and Famous." It had as one of its tag lines the phrase "This is the good life." It included such things as dinner for two that easily cost hundreds of dollars. Or a yacht that rented for several thousands of dollars a day. Or a "modest" home that sold for $6 million. This is called "the playground of the world" we were told.

But one reporter who worked on the show found some interesting facts about the people portrayed in those episodes. As he took some random pictures that could be used in promotional pieces or in advertisements, he caught one woman standing alone on a yacht staring sadly at the beach, a tear running down her cheek. Another time, he saw a man in a drunken stupor talking to himself as he lay under a bus stop bench. Other photographs revealed similar images. In an article about his photographs, the reporter summarized, "I couldn't help thinking how these people seemed to hunger and thirst for all that happiness money could buy. Then it suddenly dawned on me that they had actually found all the happiness money could buy."

Whoever or whatever serves as "Lord" of your life and mine determines the real value of life. That is why the absence of the Church's message – the Good Story – would hurt our communities and the world.

Son. Savior. Lord. These are the parts of the Good Story we as the Church must share. We must keep them always at hand.

When we, like Peter, discover the real Jesus, we are never again the same. We become another rock upon which God builds the Church. We become essential to the community where we live and the world we share. When we discover who Jesus really is, we become part of the kerygma; we become part of the "Good Story" the world needs to hear.

Koinonia

Our love to God is measured by our everyday fellowship with others and the love it displays.
Writer/teacher/pastor, Andrew Murray

It is within the reach of most of us to be something special. We can be a success or hero or superstar if we choose to be so. We can be famous or wealthy or powerful. The choice is ours. We can be everything that makes for greatness. But we cannot be whole without fellowship. Fellowship is one of the fiercest cravings of human beings. It is also one of our most vital needs.

Even God had need for fellowship. I believe this is part of the lesson of the creation story: God did not feel whole without human companionship. Author/educator/civil rights activist James Weldon Johnson helps us feel God's hunger for fellowship in his wonderful poem "The Creation." He tells us how for five days God made light and night; the stars and sun and moon. He tells us in elegant but vivid detail how God made the earth and mountains and seas. Then, plants and fowls and animals followed. After each part of creation was complete, God would lean back and say with great satisfaction, "That's good!"

But, after five days of marvelous, mind-blowing creativity God says sadly to himself, "But I'm lonely still." So God sat himself down to think and said to himself, "I'll make me a man." Then God scooped up some of the clay, made moist by the morning dew and molded, squeezed, shaped it until this crowning creation was made in God's own image. God then breathed into this lump of lifeless clay God's own breath of life to give that creature a living soul. At last, God felt complete, whole because God had Adam – and later Eve – with whom to fellowship.

Centuries later, Jesus founded the Church to be the center of continuing that fellowship. The Greeks called it *Koinonia* (koi-no-nee-ah). This koinonia carries with it several distinguishing characteristics which make it one of the essential marks of the Church and uniquely the task at hand for the Church.

FELLOWSHIP AROUND A PERSON

The first distinguishing characteristic of koinonia is that it is a fellowship centered in a person. That person is Jesus Christ.

This kind of fellowship is not political or fraternal. It does not rise out of some common kinship. Koinonia is not a forum where social graces and amenities are freely exchanged. It is not camaraderie of mutual admirers.

Koinonia is the fellowship that exists both when two or three of us are gathered in Jesus' name, and when individually we scatter in Jesus' name to witness and to work in the world God has entrusted to us. Therefore, gathered or scattered, Jesus is always the center. He is always the "party of the first part." You and I are the participants of the fellowship. We are always the party of the second/third/fourth/...part.

The world has never been able to understand or fully grasp the lingering influence of this fellowship of Jesus. Few believed that small fellowship of disoriented and disorganized disciples would ever amount to anything. After all, small bands of such people popped up regularly in that part of the world. Only to be dispersed and demolished quickly by governments and empires.

But this fellowship of disciples centered not on some idea of revolution or rebellion. It centered not on some new illusion. This koinonia centered in the person of Jesus Christ, who had already conquered death. In time, empires and governments came to deal with its strength and influence.

Across the centuries some have doubted this koinonia would permanently prevail. Voltaire, of the eighteenth century, once remarked absolute clear certainty "Ere the beginning of the 19th century and Christianity will have perished from the earth." We are now well into the 21st century and the koinonia in Christ is still going strong. Voltaire, in the meantime, has vanished from the earth. And only rarely is his name or philosophy mentioned.

This koinonia has stood the test of time not because it is founded on some principle or proposition. Rather, because it is founded on the person of Jesus.

FELLOWSHIP OF ACCEPTANCE

The second distinguishing trait of koinonia is that it is a fellowship of unmitigated acceptance. No questions are asked. No committee investigations are made. No initiation fees or performances are imposed. The image of God is all that is needed for entry. None who are a part of the koinonia deserve to be so; none who are a part have earned it. All are welcomed into the fellowship.

Such permissive requirements sound reckless, but it has to be that way. The One who is Head of this koinonia is the One who long ago welcomed the likes of outcasts, outlaws and out-of-their-minds. Utter acceptance of others is a powerful weapon.

Have you ever wondered why there are always cars and pickups around roadside bars and taverns?

Near Stanton, Tennessee, where some of my extended family live, there once was (and probably still is!) an old, run-down, falling-apart roadside bar. For many years, that old bar has stood on that corner between Brownsville and Memphis. It has been wrecked several times. It has burned to the ground on more than one occasion. It has changed names and owners and colors and shape more times that I can remember. But for all its rebuilding, repainting and renaming, it has not once improved in appearance. It sits in an awful location on a river bottom, dark and hidden behind tall elm trees and overgrown shrubs. Still, there are always cars and pickup trucks parked around it, crowded into every possible spot, often spilling onto the shoulders of the narrow road several yards away.

If you were to ask anyone who lives near that old run-down bar, or anyone who continues to go there, they will tell you it is always packed because its customers are accepted without question; all are welcomed without expectation.

It may sound sacrilegious, but there is a striking similarity in the attraction of a bar and that of koinonia. The end result is the same. In both places, the fellowship is extended without question about one's past. Or questions about one's present. Or one's pedigree. Everyone is accepted. All are included.

Many communities do not yet believe that kind of fellowship is happening in and around the Church. Perhaps they are right. But when it does happen, the church will experience congestion both of cars and people.

FELLOWSHIP OF ENCOURAGEMENT

The third trait of this koinonia is that it is a fellowship of encouragement.

Someone once said, "This is a day when even dreamers need to be encouraged." That is probably true. Many are losing hope. Some openly suggest the church is beyond revitalization. But if we can trust the teachings of history, we must know that God is constantly revitalizing the Church. History tells us that when people are most discouraged, they are most open to

God's encouragement. And by the sheer force of that encouraging word, they have climbed to new heights of power, faith and effectiveness.

No one could have been more discouraged that Peter in the Upper Room. He had declared his dying loyalty to Jesus, only to hear Jesus tell him he would deny knowing Jesus before the night was over. But then came Jesus' words of encouragement, "But when you have turned back…strengthen your brothers." Not "if" you turn back, but "when."

It is a word encouraging enough to inspire Peter to reach for the stars. It was encouragement enough for Peter to turn from a weak-kneed wimp to the Rock upon which the koinonia was built.

The prophet Isaiah speaks of encouragement in the 49th chapter of the book that bears his name. The people of Israel were in exile in Babylon. They had lost all hope. Daily their lives were drained out a bit more by the dull routine of slavery. Their weak and pathetic cry of desperation was "The Lord has forsaken us!" In rebuttal to their deepening discouragement, Isaiah said to them, "God has not forsaken you. God has written your names on the palms of his hands."

Koinonia is that experience – whether in the sanctuary or on the street – in which the discouraged hears again the words of Isaiah: "God has written your name on the palm of his hand."

Because koinonia centers in Jesus Christ, it invites all people without regard to credentials, and encourages those who are losing hope. Koinonia takes place when you and I are so overtaken by Jesus that we in turn set others on fire for Jesus.

Among Elton Trueblood's many books is his *The Incendiary Fellowship*. The title speaks to the flammable, spreading and engulfing nature of koinonia. It is both centrifugal and centripetal. It first thrusts us out into the ebb and flow of human life. Then as it draws us back in, we catch those who have lost their way, and are losing hope and bring them with us into the fellowship of welcome and encouragement.

Koinonia is one of the essential marks of the Church. It is one of the pillars of the Church our communities and the world cannot do without.

Didache

> *Love is all you need.*
> John Lennon

"What goes around eventually comes around." There seems to be some truth in that well-worn adage.

Even the Church seems subject to recurring circumstances. Though centuries have passed, the Church today finds its situation strangely similar to that of the first century Church. It still has to convince the world that its teachings are the final hope for all of humanity. The Church is still up against a majority that is frequently critical, sometimes hostile, and often deaf to what it tries to communicate. And, like the first century, the Church's task is to distribute its teachings, regardless of its audience's attitude, disposition, or level of receptivity.

These teachings, in the Greek, are referred to as the *Didache* (did-ah-kay). We do not have a single reference in Scripture which totally defines this didache. But much of it can be gathered from Jesus' conversation with the lawyer in Mark 12: 28-31. Here, the didache has to do with love. And three facets of the Church's teaching on love can be seen in this text.

YOU ARE LOVED

The first teaching is this: You Are Loved. Just three little words. But what power and possibility come from the discovery that each of us is personally loved by God.

Say to a child, "You are loved," and watch as trusting arms open to receive you. Tell your friend, "You are loved," and your friendship will be broadened and deepened. Whisper to your spouse, "You are loved," and your marriage will be refreshed and enriched.

It makes a world of difference when anyone discovers he or she is loved. To be loved is, in fact, the essential ingredient to life. Leave it out, and life will slowly shrivel and fade away. Some years ago, in my hometown, a young, vibrant seventeen-year-old homeless girl was found dead by suicide. In her hand she left a very revealing summary of why she ended her life. The note simply read, "In all my life, I have felt no one's love."

Somehow, the church failed that young woman. Somehow, the church had missed telling her "You are loved" and failed to help her know that she was always and forever in God's love.

In a pet shop over a kennel of playful puppies, there was an inviting sign that read, "Love guaranteed forever." That was God's message to that girl. But somehow, she either never saw that sign, or the church never helped her to believe it. Or perhaps both.

We cannot make it without being loved. That's why the world cannot be what God intended without the Church. It is the task of the Church to see that every person comes under the awesome awareness of God's love. Such awareness gives life its roots. It gives a sense of heritage in the family of God.

Years ago, I laughed at an article about Martha Taft. While still in elementary school in Cincinnati, she was asked to introduce herself to her classmates. She stood beside her desk and with stunning confidence declared, "My name is Martha Bowers Taft. My great-grandfather was President of the United States. My grandfather was a United States Senator. My father is Ambassador to Ireland. And I am a Brownie."

Having such an impressive pedigree would make anybody into an instant "somebody." But until our pedigree is followed with the words, "And I am loved," the whole story has not been told. Not even the best part has been told.

A few decades ago, the Lay Witness Movement taught us to say to each other, "God loves you and I love you." Some of us had a hard time with the second half of that statement. We just were not quite sure we were being honest when we said, "And I love you." We were not sure we could love someone we just met. But we are sure the first half of that statement is true. We can say, "You are loved." And in saying it, we declare the Church's vital teaching to the world.

YOU ARE TO LOVE GOD

The Church's second teaching is this: "You are to love God." As Jesus sat talking, a lawyer spoke up and asked, "Which is the first commandment?" In other words, "What is your chief teaching?" Instead of formulating some new commandment, Jesus reached all the way back to Deuteronomy and brought up the *Shema*. "The first commandment is this," he said. "You are to love the Lord your God with all your heart and with all your soul and with all your mind and with all your strength."

The teaching of the Church from that day, Jesus has said, is that we are to love God first. God holds first claim on our affections. Just as we cannot make it without being loved, so we cannot make it unless we love God first with all our faculties.

By loving God first, we are free to love boldly everything and anything we please. Augustine shook his world when he once said, "Love God and do as you please." It sounded like heresy. "Doing as you please" sounded too much like embracing the lifestyle of a prodigal child. But we soon realize if God is loved first, then that love directs what it is we are pleased to do.

When an old saint of a country church was once asked how she lived such an inspirational life, she smiled and said, "When you love God with all your being, it's easier to take what life does to you. It's easier to stand up to those things that try to bring you down."

"First love for God" was what kept her standing when pneumonia took her first husband, leaving her with small children to care for during the Great Depression. "First love for God" kept her standing when a farm accident took her second husband and their mortgaged farm. "First love for God" kept her standing strong in the faith when she was tempted to compromise her faith for the sake of financial independence.

We don't have to worry about our conduct if God holds first claim on our love. So long as we lean on our love for God, all the little gods that try to destroy us are held at bay.

In the mid-nineteenth century, Fidelea Fisk was a missionary to what is now Iran. Being in poor health, she found it unbearable to sit on the floor as was the custom for teachers instructing children. During the afternoon, one devoted student saw her beloved teacher's pain and moved to sit down behind her teacher and, with her own back, became a strong support. Sensing "Miss Fisk" was trying not to lean too heavily against her, the girl whispered, "If you love me, lean hard."

The teaching of the Church is simply this: "When you love God with all your heart, mind, soul, and strength you can lean hard on that love. That love is strong enough to hold you strong against the pain and strain of any sin or struggle."

YOU ARE TO LOVE OTHERS

The third teaching of the Church is this: "You are to love others." Having declared God to be the One who hold first claim on our love, Jesus said we are to love others as we love ourselves.

The best way to express love for God is still by loving all others. Such affection is usually expressed as deeds of service or meeting the needs of another. But, let's also think of love of others as that which we do to bring the other person closer to God.

In this farewell sermon, John Bunyan said, "Do you see a soul that has the image of God in him? Then love him. For that man and you will get to heaven together one day."

The strongest expression of our love for others is what we do to bring another closer to God. Preacher Kenneth Chaffin told of a prominent businessman in Fort Worth, Texas. He was a man of wealth and intelligence. But he found it difficult to share his faith, or to get involved directly in hands-on service ministries. He wanted to help people find the joy of the Christian faith. So, he set out to show his love for others by bringing them to church. He would say to a colleague or friend, "I have found something in church. Come with me and see for yourself."

Over the years, many responded. At his memorial service several years later, the house was packed. Chaffin said on that day at least twenty men said to him, "I am a follower of Jesus today for one reason: that man brought me here. And what I felt and what I heard here, I found to be true. So I responded."

Loving others is not just helping them through some pain or problem. It is also seeing in them the image of God and bringing them closer to God. That is the greatest of all expressions of love of others.

Love for others is not something we can keep restrained. We are not to be like the old Vermont farmer at his gold wedding anniversary celebration. Asked if he would like to say something to his lifelong mate, he replied, "Sarah, I have loved you so much these past fifty years that sometimes I could hardly keep from telling you."

Love for others cannot be silent. It must express itself in acts to help the other who is in need. But it must also express itself in bringing the other person closer to God. That's why Jesus told the story of the Good Samaritan. Not only did the Samaritan bind up the victim's wounds, he "brought him to heaven" where all his wounds were healed.

What, then, is the didache? What is the teaching of the Church that is so vital to the world? It is simple. So simple that it can be summed up in three brief sentences: You are loved by God. You are to love God first. You are to love others as you love yourself.

These teachings practiced daily make a world of difference for our lives. Practiced daily, they also make the world a better place.

Diakonia

I slept and dreamt that life was joy. I awoke and saw that life was service. I acted and behold, service was joy.
Bengali poet, Rabindranath Tagore

You can call us by our denominational names. You can call us Protestants. You can call us Christians. Call us what you will. But if you are going to call us what we are meant to be, call us "Servants." And one of the essential marks of the Church, and our task as the Church, is service. The Greeks referred to it as *Diakonia* (dee-ak-on-nee-yah).

Jesus demonstrated this diakonia in the Upper Room by washing the disciples' feet. Only a mother or slave would have done that kind of service. A mother would have washed the feet of her children for sake of love. A slave would have washed the feet of his or her master, and those of the master's household, for obedience sake.

Though the disciples sometimes displayed childlike behavior, they were no children. Nor were they slaves. Yet, Jesus got down on his knees and washed their tired, dirty feet. What made him do it? He did it to teach the disciples the very essence of diakonia. He did it to dramatize for them that one of the pillars of the Church – the Church they would be called to build – was that of service.

But what was it about Jesus' particular act of service that made it any different from so-called secular service or civil service or social service? Several characteristics in Jesus' act set it apart clearly from other expressions of service.

DRIVEN BY SELF-GIVING

Diakonia distinguishes itself from other expressions of service because it is driven by self-giving. Ordinary service is done for duty's sake. Sometimes it is done for decency's sake. Service to others is often driven by the desire for position or power or greed. But only diakonia is driven to give selflessly.

In an hour when Jesus needed to feel the strength of his disciples, he felt the urgency to give himself on their behalf. In the heat of their debate as to who was the greatest among them, Jesus was moved to clothe himself in a towel, the garb of a slave. He poured water into a basin and began washing their feet.

He would teach them the value of self-giving service. His action said to them, "Your time and energy will accomplish God's work only when your driving desire is to give yourselves for others, without regard for personal reward or safety."

When advised by close friends and family to take more time for himself, French biologist/microbiologist/chemist Louis Pasteur was reluctant. As if he were driven by some mysterious force, he answered, "My time and energy belong to humanity." His words sound strangely like Jesus when he said, "I must do the works of the One who sent me while it is day, for the night comes when no one shall work."

Pasteur, like Jesus, had his contribution to leave behind for the sake of humanity's future. Time and energy spent on himself was a misspent luxury he neither wanted nor needed.

Make no mistake about it though, service driven by self-giving is always costly. At the same time, the benefits are usually priceless. Many years ago, Bishop Frederick Fisher and his wife were in India. Hunger and shocking poverty and disease were thick everywhere they looked. Children with sad eyes, swollen bellies, and sickly bodies cried out for food, water, and someone to just touch or hold them. Sprawled on a straw mat was a small child who gazed longingly at the Bishop's wife. Her scrawny arms reached up, begging to be held. Mrs. Fisher could not resist. Burning hot with typhus fever, the little girl died in Mrs. Fisher's arms. Several days later, Mrs. Fisher was dead from the same disease. Heartbroken, the Bishop wrote the tribute to his wife's life. Her gravestone reads these words: "She died serving."

Service driven by arms and hearts reaching out for us is likely to cost us. It may even bring us to our knees to wash dirty feet. But that's the unique characteristic of diakonia. It is selfless.

TAKES THE INITIATIVE

Diakonia is also distinctive service because it always takes the initiative. It sees a need and moves immediately to meet it. Because it is driven by self-giving, it never waits for orders. It never waits for an urgency or emergency to make its move. We, then, who are called to service, live our daily lives on the cutting edge of readiness. We watch for openings to serve others in Jesus' name.

In a book entitled *Crowded Pews and Lonely People*, Marion Jacobson tells of a first grader named Jimmy who lost his father in a tractor accident. A classmate named Billy met Jimmy trudging sadly up the stairway at school, on his way to his next class. "Hi Jimmy!" Billy said as they met on the stairs. "How are you getting along?" Jimmy replied, "Oh, fine, I guess."

Billy then said, "You know, Jimmy, my parents and I have been praying for you and your mom ever since your dad was killed."

Tears dripped down Jimmy's face as Billy took him by the arm and lead him to a quiet corner near the stairs. With his chin quivering, Jimmy confessed: "You know, it was a lie when I said things were fine. Everything is just awful, really. We're having trouble with the cattle, and a lot of the farm equipment is not working right. My mother is so sad all the time. She doesn't know what to do. But I didn't know anyone was praying for us."

Diakonia takes the initiative. It reaches out to people who are trudging along and says to them, "I know you are hurting. And I know things are hard on you. But I'm here for you and we'll get through this together."

Diakonia is drawn automatically by the needs of others. It looks for the opportunity to serve another. It does not wait to be invited. Nor does it wait until the need becomes an emergency. Sometimes it doesn't even wait until the need is obvious.

I love the story of the frail old lady who could be just about anyone we know. Her frazzled shawl made her poverty obvious to all. Yet, several times a week, she could be seen stooped over gathering objects from the road that ran in front of her ramshackle home and hiding them in her apron. Someone reported her to the police as being a bit crazy and may end up getting killed or causing a terrible accident. A police officer was sent to investigate the situation and watched her for a couple of days to see what she could possibly be doing. Finally, he approached her and, with a hint of authority in his voice, said, "Old woman, what are you picking up and hiding in your apron?" Startled, but smiling, the woman opened her apron to reveal pieces of broken glass, bent nails and jagged objects. She said, "I pick up these things every few days, because so many of our children who must come down this road to go to school have no shoes. I don't want them to cut their feet."

There is diakonia made plain. It is seeing a need and moving to meeting it. It is taking the initiative, sometimes even before the need is urgent or obvious. And only the Church is in that kind of business.

IT GOES THE DISTANCE

Diakonia distinguishes itself also because it is service that goes the distance. When Jesus put on the towel and took up the basin and bent his knees to wash the disciples' feet, he went the distance. No wonder such service melted their self-centered hearts. Their Lord had gone down deep into their hearts and had called them to service.

There comes a time when social service says, "We can do nothing more." There is a point when humanitarian service is forced to say, "We can go no further." But diakonia is not finished until it has gone the distance. It is not through until it has made a difference. Diakonia is not finished until it has taken the load from someone's life and made it its own.

A new mother left her only child in the church nursery for the first time. Bravely, she left the toddler in the arms of the attendant. With a lump in her throat, and without looking back, she quickly made her way out of sight, upstairs and into the worship celebration. She sat on the back row, close to the door but was fidgety the entire time and preoccupied during the service. When worship was over, she hurried to pick up her anxious son and asked the attendant, "Did he cry a lot?" The attendant smiled and replied, "No, but his teacher did!"

Diakonia is seen even in the humor of that moment. Diakonia is going the distance by taking on someone else's most precious concern and carrying it until it can be picked up and cared for again. And through it all, it is willing to "cry a lot" for the frustration.

When we are tempted to guard our own dignity or rights or reputation, when we are tempted to think we have done enough, let's remind ourselves of Jesus, with a towel wrapped around his waist, kneeling as a servant to wash the disciples' feet.

Diakonia is the work of the Church. That work is carried out, not by uniquely gifted people, but by ordinary people like you and me who are willing to be servants of our Servant Lord.

In St. Paul's Cathedral in London, there is a memorial to General Charles Gordon. He was a faithful British officer in China, Egypt, and Sudan. He was as much known for his commitment to the faith as he was to his country. The memorial reads: "He gave his strength to the weak; his substance to the poor; his sympathy to the suffering; and his heart to God."

Any one of us can do those first three things, but only if we do the last thing first. Give your heart to God first and you are driven to serve others. Give your heart to God first and you will reach out to every person you meet who is struggling in some way in life. Give you heart to God first and you can go the distance in meeting someone's need. Give your hearts to God first and diakonia will be the first order of business in your life, today and every day.

Diakonia is the kind of service our world, our communities, our neighbors cannot do without. Without it, our world is not what God intended it to be. And that is why diakonia is one of the essential marks in the work of the Church.

Afterword

Over the course of the past several decades, much has been written and taught about leadership in the church, what the work of the Church is, and what the best way is to go about that work. Many of those books have proved to be useful. Others, not so much. As I write this, I can see one of the bookshelves in my office includes numerous such books I have bought over the years. Thumbing through them, I see where I highlighted some thought, idea, or program I believed was worth considering or putting into practice in the church I was serving at the time.

The problem with many of those leadership books (and seminars, lectures, and articles) is that far too often, we think of them as cookie-cutter techniques that apply to all churches of all sizes in all types of settings for all denominations. We think to ourselves, "If it worked there, it will surely work here." We then dive in head-first trying to force the ideas we've read or heard from another, more "successful" church onto our local setting, only to end up frustrated to discover it often doesn't work. Maybe it wasn't meant to be.

I learned the hard way years ago, that there is no "one-size-fits-all" model for a church's ministry. But I do believe there are some basic principles which can guide any church anywhere in carrying out its unique ministry wherever it is located. The principles discussed in this book are not harebrained ideas or desperate attempts to grab onto something – anything – that might help the Church be the Church. Rather, they are biblically based and, therefore, applicable to any church of any size, serving anywhere, at any time, under the banner of any denomination.

What has been shared here is a tool any church, large or small, can use as it carries out its own ministry. But before a church can carry out its ministry, we must first remember who we are as the Church. I am convinced that to get the Church's story out, we must first get the Church's story straight. We must ask ourselves some hard questions, such as: Who are we? Why are we here? What is our message to our community? How can we best serve our community?

These questions, and others, help us figure out how we as the Church can organize (or reorganize) in such a way that helps us not only know what to do, but remember just who we are as the Church, the body of Christ in our own neck of the woods.

In my thinking, the four essentials you have read about in this book do just that. The answers to the questions above are found in Jesus' teaching and in the New Testament. While they are simple in their appearance, they are not always easy in application. We know, for example, that the Church is a community, but it is not always easy to be a community with people of various backgrounds and understandings of the Church, who have gathered around the person of Jesus and invite others into that community without question.

But that's part of the beauty of the Church! While none of us is perfect, we are all in this together, striving to be what God has called us to be, encouraging one another along the way so that we can become the people – the Church – God intends us to be.

Sadly, the ideas presented herein have been forgotten or ignored in search for something easier or trendier or more appealing to a broader range of people. We have forgotten that Jesus' teachings are as timely now as they were when he first taught them, and that the scriptures express the Truth today just as they always have.

If the Church is going to remain vital and vibrant into the future, we must always remember to Whom we belong, who we are (which is answered in discovering to Whom we belong) and what the non-negotiables are in being the Church. Everything else takes second, third, fourth place. The work the Church does – its ministries and mission – are to be guided by these essential pillars: The Kerygma, Koinonia, Didache, and Diakonia. Every time a decision is being debated concerning some ministry of the church, we should ask ourselves "Does this ministry help us live out any or all of these essentials?" If the answer is "yes," then I believe the church should engage that ministry. If it happens to fail, it fails. Failure is a part of learning, a part of living. We should embrace failure and learn from it, not run from it. If, on the other hand, the answer to that question is "no," then the church should step back and rethink it, if not abandon the ministry altogether. Sometimes, the healthiest thing for a church to do is graciously allow a ministry to pass. And sometimes – oftentimes – the healthiest thing for a church to do is take a risk with the new. The failure to risk anything is to risk even greater things.

While my thoughts here are not a detailed blueprint or "how-to," I believe with all my heart that the four essentials discussed must be a part of every church's ministry; a sort of foundation from which to build each church's unique work in its unique community. My hope is that this book has encouraged and challenged you to ponder what is presented and to ask yourself and the church you call "home" the tough questions that will lead to remembering who you are as the church in your community and to better serving those who live in your zip code.

Ponder Points

Chapter 1: Kerygma

1. If your church were suddenly "blown away," who in your community would notice it missing? Why?

2. Here's a challenge: have a few of the members of your church fan out throughout your community, going to various stores, coffee shops, and other places where people gather. Without telling anyone you are a member of your church, ask those you meet if they have heard of your church and what they know about it. Then, come together with other members and discuss your findings.

3. What can you and other members of your church do to change any bad impressions or lack of knowledge of your church in your community?

4. The kerygma is not only a story we tell, it is a way we live. How do you – and the church you are a part of – live out the "kerygma," the Good Story, in your community? How has the Good Story made a difference in your life and the life of your zip code?

5. As a church, take some time to plan how you can work to share the Good Story more effectively in your community. What ministries can you offer? How can you model the kerygma in your own town? What resources are available to you and your church that would help reach your community more effectively?

Chapter 2: Koinonia

1. Do you agree or disagree that God "needed" community/fellowship? Why or why not?

2. If "koinonia" is, or can be defined as, "community" or "fellowship," what do you believe are the essentials that make up that community and fellowship?

3. In terms of how koinonia is defined in the book, how does your church exemplify "fellowship around a Person"? How does your church offer acceptance of *all* people as a part of koinonia? How does your church offer encouragement as part of its koinonia?

4. Are there ways your church fails to exemplify koinonia to your community? How? Toward whom? Why?

5. How can you and your church offer others the experience that they have not been forgotten by God; that God has written their names on the palms of God's hand?

Chapter 3: Didache

1. In the book, the author mentions that even the Church seems subject to recurring circumstances. How is the Church of today like the first-century Church? What are some other similar challenges?

2. How can you and your church show and tell your community that "You are loved"? Discuss specific examples of how you and your church have failed to show someone that he/she is loved unconditionally.

3. Do you agree or disagree with Augustine's thought that you can "Love God and do as you please"? Why or why not? Discuss or write about a time when that maxim proved true for you or your church.

4. Talk about some of the risks involved in loving God first, then loving others without restraint. What are some of the blessings of doing so? What are some of the risks?

5. What would it mean specifically for you and your church to radically love God and all others? How would that love manifest itself in your area?

Chapter 4: Diakonia

1. Do you agree or disagree with the Tagore quote at the beginning of the chapter? Why or why not? How does service bring happiness? What is the difference between happiness and joy?

2. The author claims that the Church is meant to be "servants." Do you agree or disagree? Why? If not servants, what?

3. Name a time or two when you were driven by self-giving service. How did that impact you? What about a time when you were the recipient of someone else's self-giving service?

4. When was the last time you or your church lived "on the edge of readiness," not waiting for a need to be expressed before working to meet it; you simply saw a need and immediately moved to meet it? How did that turn out?

5. Should there ever be a time when the Church says, "We've done all we can do?" When does that time come? Why?

NOTES

www.ingramcontent.com/pod-product-compliance
Lightning Source LLC
Chambersburg PA
CBHW052114110526
44592CB00013B/1607